THE MANUAL THEY NEVER GAVE US

Real Talk. Raw Truths. Revolutionary Love

By
KEVIN A. STARLINGS

© 2025 Kevin A. Starlings

All rights reserved. No part of this book may be reproduced without written permission from the author, except for brief quotations used in reviews or educational settings.

Published by

The Starlings Foundation Press — Stories That Heal. Voices That Rise.

Richmond, Virginia

ISBN 979-8-9937543-3-8 (Paperback)

Cover design and interior layout by The Starlings Foundation Press.

www.KevinStarlings.org

Printed in the United States of America.

For every parent who had to raise their children without a blueprint —
this is the manual you deserved.

TABLE OF CONTENTS

Author's Note ix
Foreword 1
How To Use This Book 3
The Manual Wasn't Missing—It Was Inside You All Along 5
Dirty Diapers, Real Tears, and Finding Out Too Late 9
Co-Parenting, Court Dates, and Calling It Quits With Class 13
Breaking Generational Curses While You're Still Healing 17
School Ain't Just for the Kids 21
Put the Phone Down: Parenting in the Age of Screens, Likes & DMs 25
The Money Talk 29
Mental Health Is Family Health 33
Discipline Without Damage: Raising Children Who Listen Without Fear . 37
From Fatherless to Fatherhood: My Journey to Showing Up Differently .. 41
Special Needs, Special Love: Raising Children with Different Abilities 45
When You Feel Like Giving Up 49
The Power of "I'm Sorry": Repairing What We Didn't Know We Broke .. 53
Faith, Hope, and the Fire It Took to Keep Going 57
The Legacy Chapter 61
Epilogue 65
About the Author 67
Acknowledgments 69

Author's Note

This book was born out of the quiet moments, the ones where I felt overwhelmed, underprepared, and unsure if I was doing anything right as a parent. It grew out of prayers whispered in the dark, mistakes I wish I could take back, victories no one saw, and the lessons that kept finding me even when I tried to avoid them.

The Manual They Never Gave Us isn't written from a mountaintop. It's written from the middle—where most of us parents are every day. These pages come from my lived experience as a father, a son, a human being still healing, learning, growing, and trying.

I wrote this book because so many of us are raising children while still raising ourselves. Because some days love feels heavy. Because there are moments when we don't know whether to cry, pray, or keep pushing. And because I believe that transparency creates room for someone else to breathe.

This is my offering. My truth. My testimony. My reminder that even without a manual, grace picks up where our strength ends.

If these pages help you feel seen, understood, or less alone, then this book has done its job.

With love and honesty,
Kevin A. Starlings

Foreword

Parenting is one of those sacred journeys we enter without a map, a blueprint, or a manual—yet somehow, we are expected to build, nurture, guide, protect, and pour out from places we ourselves are still learning to understand. *The Manual They Never Gave Us: Real Talk, Raw Truths and Revolutionary Love for Today's Parents* steps into that void with honesty, courage, and grace. It is not the typical devotional guide. It is not full of perfect answers or polished stories. Instead, it is an offering—raw, reflective, and deeply human. It is a book that dares to say the quiet parts out loud—because healing and wisdom flow freely when truth is given space to breathe.

Through Kevin Stallings' transparency, his reflections, and the intimate letters written for his children to hold onto for years to come, this book becomes more than a resource. With courage and vulnerability, he chose to share what was inside of him all along: his testimony, his wrong turns, the deaths he had to endure, the places where he bled, and the faith that carried him through it all. It becomes a companion. A reminder. A mirror. This is an invitation for every parent—new, seasoned, weary, hopeful, single, married, blended, or still figuring it out—to know that you are not alone. We all face moments when we whisper to ourselves: *How am I going to make it through this? How do I get out of this? Why didn't anybody teach me this part?*

This book stands as a reminder that parenting is not linear; it is layered. It is joy and grief, wisdom and confusion, sacrifice and surprise. It is the weight of wanting to get it right while fearing the consequences of getting it wrong. It is leaning on grace when strength runs out and trusting God when the blueprint for the moment isn't clear. Kevin speaks into that tension with a restorative gentleness, offering language for experiences many parents could never quite articulate.

The gift of this book is not that it provides a step-by-step manual, but that it affirms that the manual was always inside of you. Each devotion invites parents to pause, breathe, and realign. The journal prompts ask the questions we usually avoid—questions that open us up, stretch us, and challenge us toward growth. And the letters written to a child serve as both a love offering and a reminder: our children are not just receiving our guidance, they are receiving us—our presence, our healing, our becoming.

Kevin's story is not polished, but it is powerful. His transparency creates a space where parents can release shame, confront truth, and embrace the fullness of their journey without pretending to have mastered what none of us ever fully master. His testimony points us back to a God who parents us even as we learn to parent others—a God who guides, restores, corrects, loves, and carries us through every chapter of our lives.

I pray that as you read this book, you give yourself permission to be honest, to be vulnerable, to be human. And I pray that the reflections within these pages remind you that you are not alone, you are not failing, and you are not forgotten. Parenting is sacred, complicated, holy work. And while no one gave us a manual, God continues to give us grace—more than enough to guide us along the way.

So, as you turn these pages, don't read them as mere words. Let them become catalysts for your transformation. Let them give you permission to slow down, breathe, reflect, question, and grow. Let them remind you that mistakes do not disqualify you, that uncertainty is not failure, and that God continues to shape you as you shape the lives entrusted to your care.

—Pastor Ciarra Smith-Bond

How To Use This Book

The Manual They Never Gave Us is more than a book — it's a journey.

Every chapter includes four sections designed to help you reflect, heal, grow, and build your legacy as a parent:

Reflection – A moment to pause, breathe, and look inward.

Real Talk – Practical wisdom for real-life parenting challenges.

Journal Prompt – Space for you to write your truth, your story, and your breakthrough.

Letter to My Child – A guided moment of love — a place to speak directly to your child's heart.

Move through each chapter at your own pace. Use this book as a mirror, a guide, and a companion on your journey as a parent committed to love, healing, and legacy.

You are not alone. You are not failing.

You are building something sacred.

The Manual They Never Gave Us

Real Talk. Raw Truths. Revolutionary Love

By Kevin A. Starlings

CHAPTER ONE

The Manual Wasn't Missing—It Was Inside You All Along

I remember standing in the middle of my living room, holding a baby bottle in one hand and my phone in the other. My son was crying, I was crying, and my bank account was overdrawn by $12.74. I had no idea what I was doing—but I knew one thing for sure: I had to figure it out.

There was no hotline. No step-by-step manual. No parent handbook customized for a young Black father trying to raise a child while healing from his own childhood. I searched everywhere. Parenting books. YouTube experts. Therapy sessions. Phone calls with my mama. Conversations with people who meant well but didn't live my reality. I was looking for a rulebook that just didn't exist.

But the truth? I was the manual.

Every mistake I made taught me something. Every "I don't know what to do" moment became a turning point. I didn't have all the tools, but I had instinct. I had love. I had the unshakable will to show up. Even on the days when I felt empty, I kept showing up. And that became the greatest lesson of all: your presence matters more than your perfection.

Nobody tells you that parenting is less about knowing what to do and more about learning who you are. Your kids don't need a perfect parent—they need you, raw and real. They need your laugh, your energy, your stories, your correction, your hugs, your truth.

This chapter is about reclaiming your voice as a parent. Forget the guilt, the judgment, the comparison game. If you're still in the game, still trying, still praying for strength—you're doing it.

You are the manual.

And trust me, you're worth reading.

Reflection

I had been waiting for answers from everyone else people with more degrees, more resources, more time. But parenting isn't one-size-fits-all. It's you-sized. It's built around the imperfect love you pour into your kids every single day.

Being a parent means growing while you guide. Falling, but still reaching for your child's hand. Learning to forgive yourself while modeling what strength really looks like.

Real Talk: What You Can Do Right Now

Trust your gut. You know your child better than you think.

Give yourself grace. No parent has it all figured out.

Keep showing up. Your presence is more powerful than perfection.

Journal Prompt

When did you first feel like a real parent? Describe the moment—what were you feeling, what did you learn, and what did it teach you about yourself?

Letter to My Child

Dear My Child,

I didn't have all the answers when you came into this world. Truth is, I still don't. But I've learned that parenting isn't about knowing everything—it's about loving you through everything.

There were nights I sat in silence, wondering if I was enough. Days when I felt like the world was too heavy to carry you through. But no matter what I lacked in money, energy, or guidance—I never lacked love for you. That love became my compass.

You taught me how to be a parent. Not the kind you see on TV or read about in books, but the kind who keeps showing up—scared, tired, stretched thin—but present. The kind who learns as they lead. The kind who wipes your tears and hides their own until later.

I know I'll make mistakes. I already have. But I promise you this—I will never stop trying. Never stop learning. Never stop becoming the parent you deserve.

You are not my reason for giving up.

You are my reason for growing up.

With all my heart,

Dad

CHAPTER TWO

Dirty Diapers, Real Tears, and Finding Out Too Late

I didn't hold you in the hospital. I didn't count your fingers and toes. I didn't cut the cord or watch your chest rise and fall for the first time.

I didn't even know you existed.

That's the part people don't talk about—what it feels like to miss the beginning of your child's story. To find out you're a father not from a celebration, but from a sentence dropped like a bomb:

"He's yours."

No warning. No slow buildup. Just the weight of truth landing heavy and uninvited.

You were already walking. Saying a few words. Forming bonds I wasn't a part of. And me? I was trying to make sense of how I missed everything—your first cry, your first laugh, your first birthday.

I remember staring at you the first time we met. You looked at me like I was a stranger—and I was. I didn't know if I should smile, cry, or apologize for being late. I just knew I had to show up differently moving forward. You didn't ask to come into this world without me, and you sure didn't ask to carry the weight of my absence.

Reflection

There's no manual for being a father after the fact. The guilt eats at you. The doubt creeps in. You wonder if it's too late to make it right. You feel robbed of the memories you didn't even know you were supposed to be making.

But here's the thing I had to learn: being there now matters more than not being there then. The past hurts, but the present heals if you show up with love, consistency, and honesty.

You can't go back and change your child's beginning—but you can fight like hell to protect the rest of their story.

Real Talk: What You Can Do Right Now

Don't let shame keep you from showing up. Regret is real, but it's not a reason to stay gone.

Start where you are, with what you have. Even awkward beginnings can grow into something beautiful.

Focus on building trust, not being perfect. Love is a seed—plant it daily.

Journal Prompt

What would you say to your child about not being there in the beginning? Write it with truth and heart, even if it hurts.

Letter to My Child

Dear My Child,

I wish I had been there.

I wish I had known you were coming, that I had heard your first cry, held you when you were seconds old, kissed your forehead in the hospital. I wish I had been there for your first steps, your first birthday, your first everything.

But I wasn't. I missed all of it.

And for that, I am deeply sorry.

But I'm here now. I'm learning how to love you in real time. I'm learning how to make up for memories I can't get back by making new ones that count. I don't want to be a ghost in your story. I want to be a chapter you look back on and feel proud to have read.

You may not remember the first time I saw you, but I do. You looked at me like I didn't belong—and you were right. But I'm working every day to earn my place in your world.

I didn't get it right in the beginning. But I promise to get it real moving forward.

With all my love,

Dad

CHAPTER THREE

Co-Parenting, Court Dates, and Calling It Quits With Class

We weren't in love.

Let's be honest—we were never really together in that way. It wasn't a relationship. It was a situationship. Good times, laughs, late-night vibes that turned into a pregnancy neither of us planned.

When I found out I had a son, almost two years had already passed. The connection we once had—whatever it was—was long gone. And suddenly, we weren't just two people who used to kick it. Now we were forever connected by a child.

At first, it was chaos. Misunderstandings. Missed messages. Mixed emotions. We were trying to co-parent without trust, history, or even basic communication. That's a dangerous place to start—but it's also where many of us begin.

What followed were court dates. Paperwork. Custody conversations. Parenting plans built around people still healing from old wounds or still caught in cycles of pettiness and power. Some days felt like progress. Others, like war.

But in the middle of it all was a child. Innocent. Watching. Absorbing. Depending on us to figure it out.

That's when I had to grow up—quickly.

I had to learn to put my child's peace above my personal pride.

Reflection

It's easy to blame the other parent. To talk about what they don't do, how they move, or how things "should've" gone. But co-parenting is less about them and more about you. How you respond. How you lead. How you mature.

No one hands you a guide on how to co-parent when love never existed. But here's the truth: you can still do it with class, with clarity, and with compassion for your child.

You don't have to be best friends. You don't even have to get along all the time. But you do have to communicate, respect boundaries, and keep your child out of the storm.

Real Talk: What You Can Do Right Now

Accept what it was—and what it wasn't. Don't rewrite the past. Just grow from it.

Keep your child centered. Every decision should ask: "Does this benefit them?"

Set boundaries, not battles. Choose peace—even when it's inconvenient.

Journal Prompt

How do your personal feelings toward your child's other parent show up in your parenting decisions? What needs to shift?

Letter to My Child

Dear My Child,

You came from a moment we didn't see coming.

There wasn't a deep love story behind your arrival. There wasn't a plan or a future vision. But from the second I found out about you, everything changed.

It took me a while to find my footing. To understand how to show up for you while standing across from someone I didn't fully trust—or even really know anymore. But this isn't about us. It's about you.

And you? You are the best part of a messy situation.

I can't promise your parents will always agree. I can't promise there won't be tough days. But I can promise that I will never stop fighting to be the father you deserve. I won't let my history with your other parent define my future with you.

You're not a mistake.

You're a miracle.

And no matter how it all began, I'm thankful I get to be your Dad.

With everything I've got,

Dad

CHAPTER FOUR

Breaking Generational Curses While You're Still Healing

I wasn't raised by my biological parents.

Both of them struggled with drug addiction, and the kind of love I needed as a child wasn't something they could give. But God didn't leave me empty-handed—He gave me my grandparents.

Mama Shane and Pop were the steady hands and soft hearts that stepped in when my world could've easily fallen apart. They didn't just raise me—they loved me. They gave me safety, structure, and the kind of foundation you don't realize is sacred until you're grown and raising a child of your own.

So when people talk about "breaking generational curses," I think about it differently. Because the curse didn't live in the house I was raised in—it lived in the trauma I inherited from the bloodline I came from.

And now, as a father, I carry the tension of both:

Honoring the love that raised me, while healing from the legacy that didn't.

Reflection

Some of us weren't raised by our parents—but that doesn't mean we weren't raised right. It's possible to grow up loved and still carry pain. It's possible to be grateful and grieving at the same time. That's what makes our story complex—and powerful.

I'm not here to repeat the past. I'm here to multiply the love I was given by the ones who chose me.

Being a parent means deciding which part of your story gets to continue. And I've decided that the chaos, the abandonment, the addiction, and the silence stop with me.

My kids will know my story—but they won't relive it.

Real Talk: What You Can Do Right Now

Honor the ones who showed up. Blood makes you related, but love makes you family.

Don't confuse where you come from with where you're going.

Model what you saw in them—not what you missed from others.

Journal Prompt

Who raised you with love? What lessons did they give you that you now want to pass down to your children?

Letter to My Child

Dear My Child,

There are parts of my past I'll one day tell you about. Parts I had to grow through, cry through, and come back from. I didn't grow up with my parents—but I did grow up with love.

Your great-grandparents gave me the kind of childhood I still hold on to like a warm blanket. They didn't have to raise me—but they did. They didn't always have a lot—but they gave me everything that mattered.

That's who I want to be for you.

I don't want to pass down pain. I want to pass down peace. I want to raise you with the same hands that held me steady, the same kind of love that healed parts of me before I even knew I was broken.

You may never meet some of the people in my story, but you'll feel the impact of their love in how I parent you.

We are continuing their legacy—stronger, wiser, and with open hearts.

With all the love I was given and more,

Dad

CHAPTER FIVE

School Ain't Just for the Kids: Showing Up As Your Child's First Advocate

I used to think dropping my child off at school meant they were in good hands.

That someone would see what I saw—a bright, funny, curious child with potential written all over them. I thought teachers would naturally pour into my child, that the system would protect and nurture him. But I learned quickly: no one will fight for your child the way you will.

The first time I got called in for a "behavior issue," I felt a mix of confusion and anger. The way they described my child didn't sound like the child I knew. They used words like "disruptive," "distracted," "challenging." What they didn't say was that he was brilliant. Sensitive. Deeply observant. That he was dealing with things outside of school that most adults wouldn't know how to carry.

That's when I realized my role wasn't just about showing up at parent-teacher night. I had to stand up, speak out, and advocate—not just for grades, but for dignity. For understanding. For the right to learn without being labeled.

Reflection

The truth is, many schools weren't built to understand or affirm kids who don't fit neatly into the system. And when you're Black, brown, disabled, neurodivergent, or just different—they see behavior before they ever see brilliance.

That's why our presence matters. Because sometimes we have to translate for our children until they learn to use their own voice. Sometimes we have to show up when we're tired, write the emails, attend the meetings, push back respectfully, and remind them:

"My child is not a problem. My child is a person."

Real Talk: What You Can Do Right Now

Don't be intimidated by the system. You belong at the table—even if they never planned for you to sit there.

Learn your rights. Ask questions, read policies, and bring backup if you need it.

Document everything. Keep a record of meetings, concerns, and communications.

Speak life into your child daily. Let your child know, "No matter what they say, I see you."

Journal Prompt

When was a time you had to step up for your child in school? What did it teach you about your own power as a parent?

Letter to My Child

Dear My Child,

School can be hard. Not just the work—but the way people treat you when they don't understand your heart, your mind, or your spirit. There will be times when you're overlooked, mislabeled, or underestimated. But I want you to know this:

You are not what they call you. You are who you were created to be.

I will always stand up for you. I will walk into any room, sit across any table, and remind the world of your worth. Because I know your light. I see your gifts. And I will fight to make sure others do too.

You were never meant to fit into a system. You were meant to shine through it.

Keep being bold. Keep being you.

And know that wherever your classroom is—I'll always have your back.

With fierce love,

Dad

CHAPTER SIX

Put the Phone Down: Parenting in the Age of Screens, Likes & DMs

I grew up playing outside until the streetlights came on. We rode bikes, played tag, and talked to each other face-to-face. Our "likes" came in the form of real laughter, not double taps. Now I'm raising kids in a world where attention is currency, and comparison is constant.

It's wild.

My oldest son knows how to edit videos better than I ever could. My middle child can unlock a phone faster than I can find my glasses. And even the toddler knows how to swipe a screen. This generation is fluent in tech—but sometimes, I worry they're losing fluency in life.

There's so much noise. So much pressure to perform, post, impress. So many ways to get caught up in things that look good but feel empty.

As a father, I had to check myself first. I couldn't tell my kids to put their phones down while I was still scrolling mine every chance I got. I had to model the balance I was trying to teach.

And trust me, it's a battle. Because technology isn't the enemy—disconnection is.

Reflection

We're the first generation of parents raising kids in a fully digital world. There's no blueprint for this. We're figuring it out as we go. And while phones, apps, and social media aren't going anywhere, we can teach our kids how to navigate them without losing themselves in the process.

That means creating space for real conversations—not lectures. It means letting them see us unplug, be present, and admit when we need to do better too. It means teaching them that likes aren't love, followers aren't friends, and identity isn't built through filters.

Because the most valuable thing they'll ever be in this world… is real.

Real Talk: What You Can Do Right Now

Set boundaries, not battles. Make tech-free time a family thing, not just a punishment.

Talk about what they're watching and posting. Be curious, not controlling.

Model digital balance. Kids notice when you're distracted—even more than when you're strict.

Remind them: validation starts at home. Make sure your voice is louder than the crowd.

Journal Prompt

What's one small change you can make to be more present with your kids this week—without a screen in your hand?

Letter to My Child

Dear My Child,

The world you're growing up in is different than the one I knew. Your childhood has apps, algorithms, and attention spans shorter than commercials. I know it's hard. I know the pressure to perform, post, and keep up can feel like a race you didn't ask to run.

But hear this:

You are more than your likes. You are more than a story post. You are more than someone's opinion.

Don't let the world rush you into becoming something you're not. You don't have to be viral to be valuable. And you don't need filters to be beautiful, talented, or worthy.

I will always be your safe space—the place where you don't have to pretend, compete, or impress.

Let's both keep working on putting the phones down—and showing up for real life.

With full presence and love,

Dad

CHAPTER SEVEN

The Money Talk: Budgeting for Backpacks, Birthdays, and Broken Dreams

Nobody really talks about the money.

Not the cost of diapers that show up before your first paycheck clears. Not the birthday party you try to make magical even though your lights might get cut off the next day. Not the guilt of telling your child "maybe next time" when you're not even sure next time will come with a raise.

Money changes everything. And when you're a parent—especially one doing it alone—it can feel like every dollar you make is already spoken for before you even touch it.

I've been there.

I've raised four children—but there's something about raising a child by yourself that hits different. I've had full custody of my second son since he was two years old. That means everything—school clothes, doctor visits, daycare bills, food, toys, haircuts, emergencies—all on me.

There were times when I had to choose between gas for the car and groceries for the week. Times when my son needed a new backpack, and I was trying to stretch twenty dollars to feel like eighty. And let me be honest—there were days I felt ashamed. Ashamed that I couldn't give him what other kids had. Ashamed that no one really understood how hard I was trying.

But my son never saw shame on my face. He saw effort. He saw love. He saw someone who showed up—even when he was stretched to the limit.

That's the part we don't talk about enough:

How love shows up in every sacrifice we make.

Reflection

Money won't make you a good parent—but it will test your ability to plan, prioritize, and push through. And sometimes, our kids don't understand why we say "no" until they're old enough to realize we were saying "yes" to keeping the lights on. "Yes" to keeping the car running. "Yes" to making a dollar do the impossible.

So when you feel like you're failing because you can't give your kids everything, remember this:

You're giving them what counts—your presence, your protection, your perseverance.

That's wealth too.

Real Talk: What You Can Do Right Now

Create a basic budget—even if it hurts. Knowing where it's going gives you power.

Prioritize memories over materials. Your child will remember time, not price tags.

Ask for help when needed. There's strength in community.

Forgive yourself for not having it all. You're still giving your all.

Journal Prompt

What financial lessons do you want your child to learn from watching you? How can you model balance, not burnout?

Letter to My Child

Dear My Child,

I wish I could give you everything you ask for.

The shoes. The parties. The game consoles. The latest whatever. I wish I had it all to give—but some days, I'm giving you everything I've got just to keep things steady.

But here's what I can give you:

A home filled with love. A father who fights for your future. A life where sacrifice is the foundation, and peace is the goal.

You may not see the invisible math I do in my head every time we walk into a store. You may not know how many times I put things back on the shelf so I could afford something for you. But one day, you'll understand.

One day, you'll look back and realize that what I gave you wasn't just what I bought—it was who I became for you.

I love you deeper than any wallet could hold.

And that love? That's priceless.

With every ounce I've got,

Dad

CHAPTER EIGHT

Mental Health Is Family Health

For a long time, I thought mental health was something you only talked about when things got really bad—like breakdowns, hospital visits, or medication. I didn't grow up hearing conversations about anxiety, therapy, or trauma. If anything, I was taught to pray it away, shake it off, or push through.

But then I became a father.

And I realized… I couldn't give my kids peace if I hadn't found it myself.

There were days I showed up for them with a smile on my face and a storm in my chest. I was tired, short-tempered, and on edge—not because of them, but because I was carrying years of unspoken pain I never addressed. I didn't want to yell. I didn't want to isolate. I didn't want to shut down—but sometimes, I did.

And when I looked in their eyes after those moments, I knew something had to change.

Because the truth is:

What we don't heal, we hand down.

Reflection

We talk about feeding our kids, clothing them, protecting them—but do we talk about how our own mental health affects how we parent?

Do we talk about the weight we carry? The grief? The fear of failing? The pressure to be strong, even when we feel weak inside?

Your kids don't need a perfect parent. But they do need one who's aware—of their triggers, of their moods, of the energy they bring into the room.

And sometimes the best parenting move you can make is booking a therapy appointment. Or going for a walk. Or taking five minutes to breathe before reacting.

Mental health isn't selfish.

It's survival. It's strategy. It's love.

Real Talk: What You Can Do Right Now

Name what you're feeling. Say it out loud. "I'm overwhelmed" is a valid sentence.

Start the healing journey—even if it's one small step. A journal, a walk, a friend.

Talk about mental health openly with your kids. Let them know it's okay to not be okay.

Let them see you take care of yourself. You're showing them how to care for themselves, too.

Journal Prompt

What unhealed pain might be affecting how you parent? What would healing that part of you unlock for your family?

Letter to My Child

Dear My Child,

If I ever seemed distant, angry, or distracted—it was never about you. Sometimes, I was carrying battles inside that I didn't know how to talk about. I was doing my best to protect you from the parts of me that were still learning how to be okay.

But here's what I want you to know:

Your presence in my life saved me in more ways than I can count. You gave me a reason to heal. A reason to grow. A reason to believe that I could break the cycle and be better—not just for you, but for me too.

I want you to know that asking for help is strength. That crying doesn't make you weak. That joy is your birthright, and peace is something worth fighting for.

You don't have to carry the same weights I did.

And I promise to do everything I can to keep them from falling on your shoulders.

We're building a healthy legacy.

Mind, body, and soul.

With clarity, courage, and love,

Dad

CHAPTER NINE

Discipline Without Damage: Raising Children Who Listen Without Fear

I used to think raising your voice meant raising a strong child. That yelling meant authority. That discipline meant control. That's what I saw growing up—in homes, in schools, even in church.

But then I became a father.

And I started to see my child flinch when my tone shifted. I started to see the fear in his eyes when I walked into the room upset. I saw what many of us never say out loud—that discipline, without care, becomes damage.

I don't want my kids to obey me out of fear. I want them to trust me enough to listen. I want them to feel safe even when they've messed up. I want them to learn right from wrong without shrinking in shame.

And that meant I had to change—not just how I parent, but how I heal.

Because the way we were disciplined growing up wasn't always love—it was survival. And survival doesn't always know the difference between correction and control.

Reflection

Discipline is not about control—it's about connection. It's not about breaking your child's will—it's about building their wisdom.

When we yell, hit, or shame, we're not teaching—we're transferring our unprocessed pain. And while it might get results in the short term, it often leaves wounds that last far longer.

Children don't need to be scared to behave. They need to feel safe enough to learn.

This chapter isn't about being soft—it's about being strong enough to discipline with love, consistency, and clarity.

Real Talk: What You Can Do Right Now

Replace reaction with reflection. Pause before disciplining—what do you want them to learn?

Use consequences that teach, not terrify. Discipline should leave lessons, not bruises—emotional or physical.

Apologize when you get it wrong. It doesn't make you weak—it shows strength and models accountability.

Separate the child from the behavior. "You made a bad choice" hits differently than "You are bad."

Journal Prompt

How were you disciplined as a child? How has that shaped the way you respond to your own children—and what are you choosing to do differently?

Letter to My Child

Dear My Child,

There will be times when you fall short. When you push boundaries. When you make decisions that I have to correct. But I want you to know this:

My love for you will never be on the line.

I will never discipline you from a place of anger or shame. I will correct you because I love you too much to let you stay in a place that harms your future. But I will never use fear to shape your heart.

You are growing, learning, becoming—and I'm here to walk with you through every mistake, every lesson, every redirection. We will grow together.

You don't have to fear me to learn from me.

And you don't have to be perfect to be worthy of grace.

Always with love and truth,

Dad

CHAPTER TEN

From Fatherless to Fatherhood: My Journey to Showing Up Differently

I didn't grow up with my biological father in the picture. He wasn't there to show me how to tie a tie or how to treat a woman. He wasn't there to teach me how to handle my emotions, manage money, or walk with confidence as a man. The silence of his absence shaped me in ways I didn't fully understand until I became a father myself.

And when I did, I was scared. Not just of failing—but of repeating him.

What if I left too?

What if I couldn't do better?

What if my kids looked at me with the same questions I had?

But that's when I made a choice—one that changed everything:

I would become everything I needed.

Not to prove something to the world. Not to get a trophy or praise. But to build the family I wished I had. To be the voice I needed. The presence I deserved. The love I longed for.

From fatherless to fatherhood wasn't a smooth path. It came with doubts. With triggers. With days I didn't feel qualified. But each time I chose to show up, I rewrote a part of the story that was once written in absence.

Reflection

When you grow up without a father, you carry questions that don't always have answers. But showing up as a father yourself doesn't mean having it all figured out—it means being willing to stay in the room, even when it's uncomfortable.

You don't have to be your past.

You don't have to be your pain.

You get to choose your legacy.

And every time you hug your child, apologize, protect, guide, and love—you are breaking the silence your father left behind.

Real Talk: What You Can Do Right Now

Acknowledge the pain. You can't fix what you won't face.

Forgive without excusing. Release the weight—even if they never say sorry.

Parent from presence, not pain. Your child isn't your childhood.

Celebrate your growth. Every day you stay is proof that you're doing it differently.

Journal Prompt

What did you need most from your father growing up? How are you becoming that for your child today?

Letter to My Child

Dear My Child,

I didn't have the roadmap. I didn't have the example. I didn't grow up watching what love from a father was supposed to look like.

But I have you.

And because I have you, I'm learning how to give what I never received.

You don't have to carry my father's absence. You don't have to feel the void I felt. Because I am here. Flawed, learning, growing—but here.

You are not growing up fatherless.

You are growing up father-filled.

And every time I show up, I'm choosing to end the cycle.

With you, I begin a new legacy.

All in, always,

Dad

CHAPTER ELEVEN

Special Needs, Special Love: Raising Children with Different Abilities

When people hear the phrase "special needs," they often think of limits. Of labels. Of everything a child can't do. But when I hear it, I don't think about limits—I think about layers.

I think about depth, sensitivity, resilience, and brilliance that doesn't always show up on a test or in a traditional classroom.

Raising a child with different abilities—whether it's developmental, emotional, or neurological—requires a different kind of strength. A different kind of patience. A different kind of love. And it changes you.

I've sat in meetings where educators used clinical terms to describe a child I saw as beautiful, creative, and complex. I've been handed reports that pointed out challenges but never highlighted how hard my child tries. I've watched my son struggle in spaces that weren't designed for his brilliance to thrive.

And through it all, I had to become his translator, his advocate, his voice—until he found his own.

Reflection

When you're raising a child with different abilities, you learn quickly that your job isn't to "fix" them—it's to fight for them. Not to make them fit into a system—but to make the system see them as they are: whole, worthy, and capable.

You start redefining success. You celebrate things others take for granted—eye contact, words spoken clearly, staying regulated in a moment that used to trigger meltdown. You become fluent in small victories.

You also grieve. Grieve the expectations the world hands out so easily. Grieve the spaces that weren't built with your child in mind. But then you rise. And you rebuild—with love as your compass and acceptance as your foundation.

Real Talk: What You Can Do Right Now

Learn the language. Understand IEPs, evaluations, and your rights as a parent.

Build a team. You need educators, therapists, family, and faith—this isn't a solo mission.

Practice grace with yourself. You're not failing—you're navigating a world that rarely offers maps.

Celebrate progress—not perfection. Every step forward counts.

Journal Prompt

What is something your child has taught you about patience, perspective, or unconditional love that you didn't understand before becoming their parent?

Letter to My Child

Dear My Child,

You are not a diagnosis.

You are not a challenge.

You are not too much.

You are a gift.

A teacher.

A miracle in motion.

I know this world hasn't always made room for you. I know there are days it feels loud, unfair, and overwhelming. But you're not alone. I see you. I advocate for you. And I will fight for you—every single day.

Your journey may look different from others, but your light? Your light is unmatched. You don't need to be like anyone else. You were created to be you—exactly as you are.

And I wouldn't change a single thing about you.

With fierce, protective love,

Dad

CHAPTER TWELVE

When You Feel Like Giving Up (But Can't)

I've had moments where I wanted to walk away. From the noise. From the pressure. From the disappointment. From the weight of trying to hold up an entire household, maintain peace, and still show up with a smile.

But every time I came close to giving up, something small reminded me why I couldn't.

A laugh from my child.

A late-night "I love you, Dad."

A hug around my waist that didn't ask for anything but closeness.

See, people talk about how strong parents are—but they rarely talk about how tired we get. How drained. How invisible. Especially when you're doing it solo, or with limited support, or while carrying trauma that hasn't fully healed.

There were nights I cried after the kids went to bed. There were mornings I got out of bed because I had to, not because I felt like it. And there were days I questioned whether I was even making a difference at all.

But giving up? It was never really an option.

Because my kids don't just need me when I'm strong. They need me when I'm real. And I've learned that being present in the storm is sometimes the most powerful thing you can do.

Reflection

Parenting will test every part of you—your patience, your faith, your finances, your mental health, your identity. And it's okay to admit when you're at your breaking point.

But just because you're tired doesn't mean you're failing.

Just because you cry doesn't mean you're weak.

Just because you think about giving up doesn't mean you will.

We don't talk enough about the strength it takes to stay—to keep showing up with empty hands but a full heart. That kind of love is holy.

And when you feel like you've got nothing left, remember this:

Love is enough. Even when you feel like you're not.

Real Talk: What You Can Do Right Now

Name your exhaustion. Let someone you trust know you're not okay.

Ask for help. It doesn't make you weak. It makes you wise.

Do one thing just for you. A breath. A walk. A journal entry. A moment.

Look at your kids. Not for pressure—but for purpose. You're not doing this for nothing.

Journal Prompt

What keeps you going on your hardest days? What message would you write to yourself right now, from the part of you that refuses to give up?

Letter to My Child

Dear My Child,

There are days when this world feels heavy. When I feel like I'm not enough. When the pressure to provide, protect, and guide you makes me question whether I'm doing anything right.

But then I see you.

And I remember why I stay in the fight.

You don't need a perfect parent. You need a present one. You need someone who chooses you—even when they feel like they're falling apart. And I do. Every time.

You may never know how many times I wanted to give up but didn't—because of you. You are the reason I wipe my tears, take a deep breath, and try again.

You are the reason I keep going.

Always and forever,

Dad

CHAPTER THIRTEEN

The Power of "I'm Sorry": Repairing What We Didn't Know We Broke

There were moments I got it wrong. Times I yelled when I should've listened. Times I punished without pausing. Times I reacted from stress, not love. And in those moments, I thought the damage was done—until I learned that one simple phrase could start to repair what I had unknowingly broken:

"I'm sorry."

Growing up, I didn't hear adults apologize to children. Authority was law. Apologies were weakness. You were supposed to "get over it" and keep moving. But when I became a father, I saw firsthand how powerful it was to simply admit when I messed up.

Because no matter how much we love our kids, we're still human. And humans hurt each other—even the ones we'd give our lives for.

But that's not the end of the story.

Healing begins with honesty.

Reflection

Saying "I'm sorry" doesn't erase the pain—but it does acknowledge it. And sometimes, that acknowledgment is what a child needs more than anything.

It Says:

"I see you."

"I value your feelings."

"You matter to me, even when I mess up."

Apologizing to your child doesn't diminish your authority—it deepens your connection. It models accountability. It teaches them that real love includes ownership and repair.

Our children don't need us to be perfect. But they do need to know that when we hurt them—intentionally or not—we care enough to make it right.

Real Talk: What You Can Do Right Now

Apologize when you're wrong. Do it clearly, and without excuses.

Make space for their feelings. Let them speak—even if it's hard to hear.

Reflect on patterns. What do you keep doing that might be hurting your child without realizing it?

Model repair. Teach your child that love is honest and humble—not prideful.

Journal Prompt

What is something you wish an adult had apologized to you for when you were younger? How can you make sure your child never has to wonder if you care enough to say "I'm sorry"?

Letter to My Child

Dear My Child,

There have been moments when I got it wrong. When I was too harsh. Too impatient. Too distracted. And even though it was never my intention, I know I may have hurt you.

So this is me saying:

I'm sorry.

I'm sorry for the moments I didn't listen when you needed to be heard.

I'm sorry if I made you feel small when you were just trying to be seen.

I'm sorry for not always giving you the grace I ask for myself.

But I'm not just sorry—I'm learning. I'm growing. I'm becoming the kind of parent you deserve. And I want you to always know: your voice matters. Your feelings matter. You matter.

And I will always fight to be better—for you.

With love and accountability,

Dad

CHAPTER FOURTEEN

Faith, Hope, and the Fire It Took to Keep Going

People see the dad at drop-off. The one cheering from the sidelines. The one showing up at school meetings, wiping tears at bedtime, teaching lessons through action. But what they don't always see is the fire it took to get here.

The kind of fire that doesn't just warm—you feel it in your bones. The kind that burned through disappointment, heartbreak, shame, and sleepless nights. The kind that came from faith that something better had to exist, even when I couldn't see it yet.

I've walked through seasons where I had nothing left but belief. No plan. No fallback. Just a whispered, "God, help me," and a commitment to not quit—even when quitting felt easier.

It wasn't always pretty. It wasn't always spiritual in the way church folks talk about. Sometimes it was survival faith. Exhausted faith. Angry faith. But it was still faith. And that seed was enough to keep going.

Because when everything else broke down—money, support, even my own confidence—hope stayed standing.

Reflection

Faith doesn't mean you never doubt. Hope doesn't mean you don't cry. And fire doesn't mean you always feel strong. It just means you refuse to go out.

You don't have to be the perfect parent to be a purposeful one. You just have to keep going. One day at a time. One prayer at a time. One decision at a time to show up, grow, and believe that what you're building matters—even when it feels invisible.

There were days I had to talk to God through clenched teeth. But I still talked. And somewhere in that pain, He gave me just enough peace to make it to tomorrow.

Real Talk: What You Can Do Right Now

Reignite your why. Write it down. Post it up. Remember who and what you're fighting for.

Feed your spirit. Whether it's prayer, scripture, meditation, or silence—tend to your inner life.

Protect your hope. Not everyone will understand your journey—and that's okay.

Don't wait until you feel strong to move. Faith works in motion.

Journal Prompt

What has kept your fire going in your lowest moments? How has faith or hope shaped the way you show up as a parent, even when everything else feels uncertain?

Letter to My Child

Dear My Child,

You are the reason I kept going.

When everything around me said "give up," I looked at you—and chose to believe that love was stronger. I chose to believe that there was something greater waiting on the other side of the pain. I chose you.

There were nights I prayed over your sleeping body, asking God to help me be what you needed. There were mornings I woke up without a clue how we'd make it—but we did.

And it wasn't because I had all the answers.

It was because I had faith.

It was because I had hope.

And it was because I had a fire in me that refused to let go of the dream of giving you more.

I love you with a strength that was forged in struggle.

And I'll never stop fighting for the future we're building—together.

With faith, fire, and forever love,

Dad

CHAPTER FIFTEEN

The Legacy Chapter: What Do You Want Them to Say About You Later?

When the noise fades.

When the toys are boxed up.

When they've moved out, started their lives, and only come home on holidays...

What will your children say about you?

Will they remember the rules—or the reasons behind them?

Will they recall the lectures—or the love that followed?

Will they say you were always right—or that you were always there?

I used to think legacy was about wealth, titles, achievements—something big enough to be carved in stone. But now I know legacy is built in the quiet, ordinary moments:

Packing lunches.

Showing up for games.

Sitting on the edge of the bed listening to stories that didn't quite make sense but mattered anyway.

Saying "I love you" even when they pushed you away.

Legacy isn't what we leave behind—it's what we plant within. And I want mine to be rooted in presence, patience, truth, and love.

Reflection

You're writing your legacy every single day.

Not with grand gestures, but with daily choices:

To stay.

To listen.

To love without condition.

To break what needed breaking and build what needed building.

Your children may not remember everything you said, but they'll never forget how you made them feel. That's your legacy.

Real Talk: What You Can Do Right Now

Write your eulogy while you're still living. What do you hope they'll say about you? Start becoming that now.

Record your values. What matters most to you? Teach it. Live it. Repeat it.

Create memory anchors. Small, intentional traditions or sayings that your kids will never forget.

Show them what love looks like—even when it's hard. Especially when it's hard.

Journal Prompt

If your child stood up to speak about you 20 years from now, what do you hope they'd say? What would make you proud to hear?

Letter to My Child

Dear My Child,

One day, you'll be older. Maybe a parent yourself. Maybe navigating your own life, your own questions, your own storms.

And I won't always be there to guide you in real time.

But my hope is that I'll still live in the way you love…

In the way you forgive…

In the way you show up when it matters most.

I hope you'll say I was patient when it was easier not to be.

That I told you the truth, even when it was uncomfortable.

That I admitted my mistakes and made space for yours.

I hope you'll feel how deeply you were loved—on the best days, and the worst.

I hope you'll remember my hugs. My lessons. My laughter. My faith.

And I hope you'll never question whether you were enough. You were. You are. You always will be.

That's my legacy.

That's my gift to you.

And it's been the honor of my life to be your Dad.

With legacy and love,

Dad

Epilogue

This Is Not the End

If you made it to this page, let me tell you something:

You are the kind of parent this world needs.

Not because you have all the answers.

Not because you always get it right.

But because you care enough to try.

You've cried.

You've questioned.

You've doubted yourself.

But you're still here—still showing up, still learning, still leading with love. That's the real work. The holy work.

I didn't write this book because I'm perfect. I wrote it because I've failed, and forgiven, and fallen, and still found my way back to love every time. I wrote it because I know what it's like to feel lost while leading little ones who think you're invincible.

So, here's what I hope you carry from these pages:

- You are allowed to grow while raising others.
- You are not your past.
- You are more than your worst moment.
- Your presence has power.
- You are already the manual.

And if you ever forget that, I hope you'll come back to this book and hear these words again:

You've got this. You're not alone. And you're worth reading.

This is not the end.

It's just a pause... before your next chapter.

With love, truth, and solidarity,

Kevin A. Starlings

Father • Entrepreneur • Advocate • Educator • Author

About the Author

Kevin A. Starlings is a father, educator, entrepreneur, advocate, and author whose work centers on resilience, equity, and the transformational power of love. With over fifteen years of experience in education, community development, nonprofit leadership, and social impact, Kevin has become a trusted voice for parents, youth, and families navigating complex realities.

As the Founder and Executive Director of The Starlings Foundation—a Richmond-based 501(c)(3) dedicated to education reform, wellness, and equitable opportunity—he leads programs that uplift youth and adults of all abilities. His leadership has earned him numerous awards, including the distinguished Hometown Hero Award for his service to the City of Richmond.

Kevin has proudly served as Chair of the Richmond Public Schools School Health Advisory Board (SHAB) and as a Community Advisory Board Member for VCU's Hydrate RPS Initiative, a national NIH-supported project advancing water equity. A proud Panther of Virginia Union University, he has studied Special Education, Business, and Psychology, blending academic insight with lived experience in his work.

Beyond his professional accomplishments, Kevin's greatest joy is being a devoted father to his four children—Jaquae, Jaylin, Jamari, and Janiyah. His life and work are rooted in faith, family, and the belief that second chances create new legacies.

The Manual They Never Gave Us is part of Kevin's growing body of work designed to heal, empower, and inspire. To learn more or connect, visit **www.KevinStarlings.org**.

Acknowledgments

To my children—Jaquae, Jaylin, Jamari, and Janiyah—you are the heartbeat of this book. Every page is a piece of our story, and every word is wrapped in the love I have for you. Thank you for teaching me more about life, love, and legacy than any textbook ever could.

To my grandparents, Mama Shane and Pop—your love raised me, your values shaped me, and your example still leads me. Thank you for showing me that presence is the greatest gift a parent can give.

To my pastor, Pastor Ciarra Smith-Bond—thank you for covering me in prayer, speaking life into me when I felt empty, and reminding me that God still writes beauty out of broken places. Your wisdom, compassion, and spiritual grounding carried me through seasons I didn't think I'd survive. I'm grateful for your leadership and your love.

To the solo parents, the co-parents, the foster parents, the grandparents raising grandkids, and every caregiver doing the work with full hearts and tired hands—this book was written for you. Your quiet strength is sacred.

To every educator, therapist, caseworker, and advocate who fights for our children when systems don't—thank you. You are part of this legacy too.

To the village that helped me grow while I was raising children—thank you for seeing me, holding me accountable, and reminding me that healing and fatherhood can coexist.

And to the reader: thank you for trusting me with your time, your heart, and your hope. You are not alone. You never were.

www.ingramcontent.com/pod-product-compliance
Lightning Source LLC
Chambersburg PA
CBHW030225170426
43194CB00007BA/861